COUNT WORM

First published in 1976
This edition published in 2016 by Hodder Children's Books

Hodder Children's Books
An imprint of Hachette Children's Group
Part of Hodder & Stoughton
Carmelite House
50 Victoria Embankment
London
EC4Y 0DZ

An Hachette UK Company
www.hachette.co.uk

A catalogue record of this book is available from the British Library.

ISBN: 978 1444 92522 7
10 9 8 7 6 5 4 3 2 1

Printed in China

MIX
Paper from
responsible sources
FSC
www.fsc.org   FSC® C104740

COUNT WORM

Roger Hargreaves

Hodder
Children's
Books

A division of Hachette Children's Group

Once there was a worm.

William, the Counting Worm!

One morning he went out for a walk. He met a small boy. The boy was crying.

"What is the matter?" asked William Worm kindly. "Why are you crying?"

"I cannot count," sniffed the boy.

"Now, now," said William Worm. "Would you like me to teach you how to count?"

"Oh yes, please," said the boy. He stopped crying.

"Very well," said William Worm.
"Let us begin."

"Now," said William Worm, "let me ask you a question. How many noses do you have on your face?"

The boy tried to look at his nose.

"One," he said, "I have one nose on my face."

"Correct," said William Worm. "Do you know what a one looks like?"

"No," said the boy.

"It looks like me," said William Worm.

William Worm went on. "Let me ask you another question. How many feet do you have?"

The boy looked down at his feet. It was easier than trying to look at his nose! "I have two feet," he replied.

"Correct," said William Worm. "You do have two feet. In fact, you have two feet more than me!" Then, he turned himself into a two.

"Is that what a two looks like?" asked the boy.
"Yes," smiled William Worm.

"What comes after two?" asked William Worm.

"I do not know," said the boy.

"Three," said William Worm. "Three comes after two. Two comes after one."

"Oh," said the boy.

"Look over there," said William Worm. "In that field there are three trees."

And he turned himself
into a three.

"One, two, three,"
said the boy.

"Correct," replied
William Worm.

"Then comes four," he continued. "There are four birds sitting on that branch. Count them."

"One, two, three, four," counted the boy.

"Great," smiled
William Worm.
He had already
become a four.

They came to a farm gate. "How many bars does that gate have?" asked William Worm.

The boy climbed up the gate. "One, two, three, four, five."

"This is what a five looks like,"
said William Worm.

They went through the farm gate. They came to a field.

"How many clouds are there in the sky?" asked William Worm.

"One, two, three, four, five, er… what comes next?" asked the boy.

"Six," replied William Worm.

They saw a farmhouse. "How many doors?"
asked William Worm.

"One," said the boy.

"And how many chimneys?"

"Two," said the boy.

"Correct," replied William Worm.

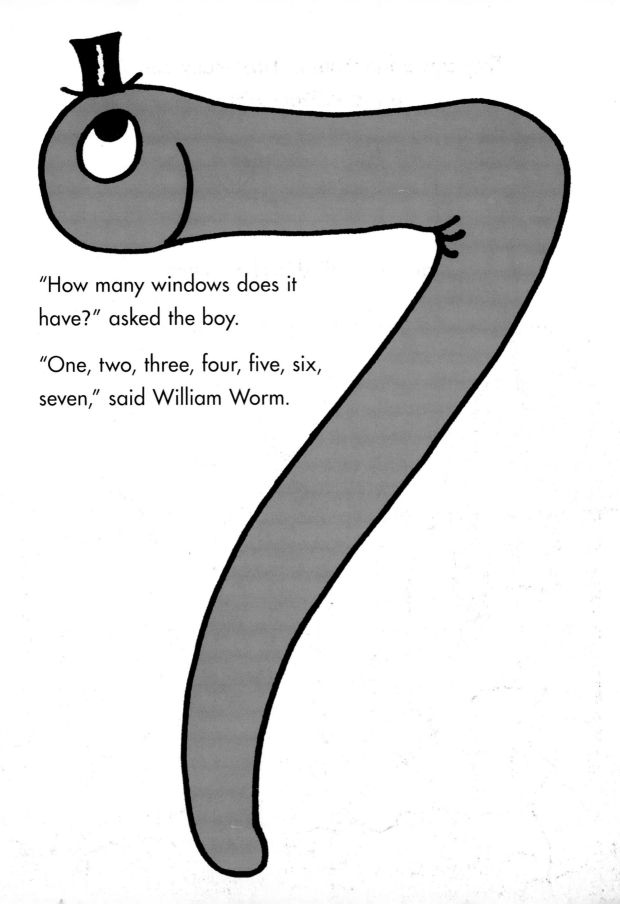

"How many windows does it have?" asked the boy.

"One, two, three, four, five, six, seven," said William Worm.

"After seven comes eight,"
said William Worm. "One,
two, three, four, five, six, seven,
eight. Do you like the flowers
over there?"

"One, two, three, four, five,
six, seven, eight flowers,"
said the boy.

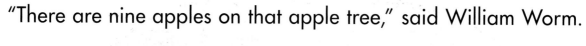

"There are nine apples on that apple tree," said William Worm.

"No, there are not," said the boy. And, he picked one of the apples and ate it! "Now there are only eight apples," he said.

William Worm smiled. He turned himself
into a nine. "You have learned
how to count,"
he said.

"One, two, three, four, five, six, seven, eight, nine," said the boy. "What comes after nine?"

"Ten," replied William Worm.

"Will you turn yourself into a ten for me?" asked the boy.

"Sorry," said William Worm,
"I can't do that alone.
I will need a friend
to help."

William Worm whistled.
It was a very loud whistle.

Another worm appeared out of the ground.
"Bobby," said William Worm.
That was the other worm's name.
"Will you help me make a ten?"

"My pleasure," said Bobby.

They made a ten.

"Thank you very much, Bobby," said the boy.

"My pleasure," replied Bobby. Then he disappeared into the ground.

"Thank you," the boy said to William Worm. He started for home. On the way he counted. "One, two, three, four, five, six, seven, eight, nine, ten."

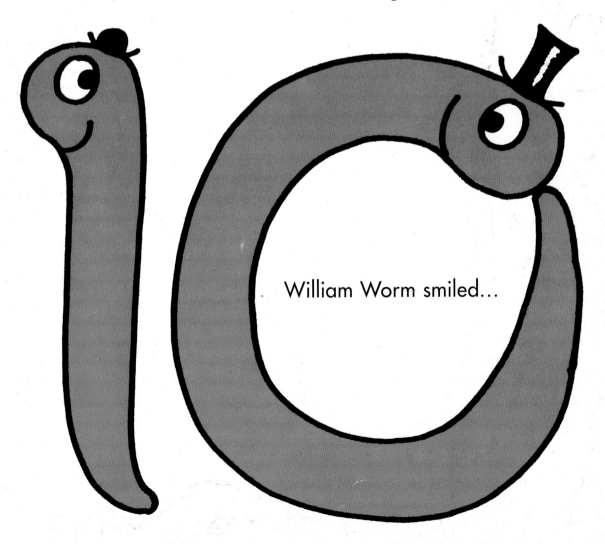

William Worm smiled...

...and crawled off.

Praise for **COUNT WORM:**

'The ultimate in simple text combined with clear colour illustrations.' **Sunday Telegraph**

Roger Hargreaves is one of the most loved children's authors and illustrators of all time, and his **Mr. Men**™ series has sold over 100 million copies.

Have you read all of these classic books?